CONTEN

CW01509256

INTRODUCTION

Where do I find joy at Christmas?

Of course, in the good news of the birth of Jesus.

Of course, in the worship offered to God in the glorious setting of Salisbury Cathedral where I live and serve as Dean.

Of course, in the carols and in the readings.

But also ... in the other stuff. The stuff we're probably not meant to talk about in church.

You know. The Christmas tree. The presents. THE FOOD.

The trips and the treats. I look forward to them. I love them. They give me **joy**.

At Christmas we celebrate the divine becoming visible in the earthly, don't we? Isn't it just possible that in this other stuff – this decidedly earthly stuff – we catch glimpses of the divine? I believe that it is.

So in these twelve meditations – with a prayer for each day and a question to wrestle with – I will introduce you to the Christmassy stuff that brings me joy. This is the stuff that opens my eyes ever wider to the mystery and wonder of Christ's birth, and my hope is that, whatever brings you joy this Christmas, it might open your eyes ever wider to that mystery and wonder, too. For ' ... *the Word became flesh and lived among us*'.

Nicholas Papadopulos
Dean of Salisbury

CHRISTMAS DAY
The Christmas Pudding

Jesus Christ is the same yesterday and today and for ever.

Hebrews 13.8

What is your favourite accompaniment? Brandy butter? Clotted cream? Both make an appearance on our dinner table, their purpose to enhance the stickily gorgeous wonder that is Christmas Pudding. Enveloped in blue flame, served as belts are being loosened, the arrival of the pud is a moment to savour.

It's also a moment to reflect. Every year, just before Advent arrives, these words are prayed in church: *'Stir up, O Lord, the wills of your faithful people ... '* It's my annual cue to go home, get stirring, and make the pudding. And then – I store it.

For thirteen months. The pud we tuck into on Christmas Day is always one made the previous year. It's been maturing. Improving in texture and flavour.

Making Christmas Pudding is an act of faith. None of us knows what the next day will bring, let alone the next twelve months. But, sitting in its dark cupboard, the pudding bears witness to a conviction that – despite the unknowable future – the story of the shepherds and angels will still be told, and Christ's birth will be celebrated. The months slip by; Christmas returns; we grow older; yet Jesus Christ is unchanging and unchangeable. He is the same, yesterday, today, and for ever. Today the timeless one enters time – and so time itself is redeemed.

What changes do you expect before you next celebrate Christmas? What might you do today that will signal your faith in God's tomorrow?

Holy God, in Mary's child you enter the world. In him all our yesterdays and all our tomorrows are one eternal present, known to you, redeemed through you, loved by you. May our changing lives be shaped by his unchanging life, this Christmastide and always. Amen.

BOXING DAY
Boxing Day Chutney

The angel said to the shepherds, 'This will be a sign for you: you will find a child wrapped in bands of cloth and lying in a manger.'

Luke 2.12

Cold meat is an annual fixture on Boxing Day. Turkey; ham; beef; whatever's in the fridge. No one has the energy to cook after the rigours of yesterday. But what turns leftovers into a feast is what accompanies them. Crispy bread. Pungent cheese. And, in our household, chutney.

Chutney-making invariably brings together a host of ingredients and flavours, most notably sugar and vinegar.

These are polar opposites: one, cloyingly sweet; the other, breathtakingly sour. Yet combine them in a pot, add fruit, add spices, cook ... and the most delicious combination emerges, a perfect marriage of different tastes.

Surely that's what we're celebrating at Christmas? Heaven and earth. Divinity and mortality. Eternity and fragility. Polar opposites, brought together and brought to birth, not diminishing one another, but creating a perfect whole. A heaven-sent child is wrapped in earthly bands of cloth. In the manger the uncreated is created. A new thing is done. And because a new thing is done, because heaven has stooped to earth, we can be hopeful.

In the child in the manger radical difference is brought together and perfect harmony is achieved. What differences need to be reconciled within you?

Holy God, in Mary's child you enter the world. You come to heal our division. For nothing can separate us from you and nothing should separate us from one another. Help us today to break down barriers, to seek peace, to foster unity. Amen.

27 DECEMBER
The Chocolate Selection

And the Word became flesh and lived among us, and we have seen his glory, the glory of a Father's only son, full of grace and truth.

John 1.14

It's one of the first signs that Christmas is coming.

Colourful plastic tubs of chocolates appear in the supermarkets, stacked high on pallets, their prices discounted, all in an attempt to lure us. They are handed around the places where we work; they are placed on shop counters to numb the bitterness of our mounting bills; they are dipped into as we slump in front of the week's TV schedule.

These Christmas chocolates are often miniature versions of the chocolate bars we buy throughout the year. Smaller, lighter, but packaged identically and with the same mixture of biscuit, caramel, honeycomb, whatever …

Now St John (whose feast day falls today) writes of the Word becoming flesh. In Jesus the true expression of God's character is revealed; the perfect articulation of God's purpose is offered. But – rather like our Christmas chocolates – in miniature! Mary's child is God through-and-through: nestling in a manger rather than a plastic tub; wrapped in swaddling clothes rather than shiny foil; but as fully God. Small, yes; diminished; no. It's extraordinary.

This seasonal miniature comes to share our life – and will never leave us. In the mystery that is unwrapped every Christmas is our eternal hope.

**How might you reveal Jesus to someone today?
It might be through the smallest gesture
or the simplest phrase.**

Holy God, in Mary's child you enter the world. Jesus is God's Word, come to live among us, to show us who our Father is, and to teach us how to love. We bow down, we worship in awe and wonder. Amen.

28 DECEMBER
Panto Season

... while gentle silence enveloped all things, and night in its swift course was now half gone, your all-powerful word leapt from heaven.

Wisdom 18.14-15

'HE'S BEHIND YOU!!!'

I love the pantomime. In fact, I love it so much that my family are reluctant to accompany me on theatre trips at Christmas!

Every pantomime tells a well-known story afresh, with topical gags that root it in the present. Every pantomime introduces us to a familiar cast: a fairy godmother; a villainous baddie (boo!); a hero and a heroine.

Every pantomime (spoiler alert unnecessary) has a happy ending, usually a wedding.

Another seasonal performance is the nativity play. It too tells a familiar story rooted (via our children's innocent faces) in the present; it too has a familiar cast (tea towels = shepherds; fairy wings = angels); and it, too, has a happy ending (*Away in a Manger*).

St John's Gospel (from which we read yesterday) speaks of God's Word becoming flesh. Today, the poet-author of The Book of Wisdom writes of God's word 'leaping' from heaven, making a dramatic entrance into the world, stepping into the spotlight. What a vision! God's Word wears no costume; his human flesh is the same as ours. There is no magic spell to save the innocent from suffering; he will die a human death. But there will be the happiest of endings: our eternal redemption through his living, and dying, and rising again.

What in your Christmas entertainment is pointing you to the story of God's incarnation and God's saving love?

Holy God, in Mary's child you enter the world, not as make-believe, but as the Truth, for it is your loving purpose that we should share your eternity. We offer you not our excited cheers – but our humble thanks. Amen.

29 DECEMBER
Christmas Jumpers

... You knit me together in my mother's womb ...
I thank you, for I am fearfully and wonderfully made ...

Psalm 139.12-13

Admit it. Do you own – or have you ever worn – a Christmas jumper? I do, and I have. They are unavoidable. They have landscapes of antlers, snowflakes, and fir trees. They feature puddings, stars, penguins, snowmen and even dinosaurs. They have jingling bells and flashing lights. They sparkle and flash. They come in the most lurid colours and questionable fabrics imaginable.

But what on earth does an item of knitwear bearing the words *'Believe In Your Elf'* and decorated with unicorns, sleigh rides, and shiny baubles have to do with what Christians celebrate at Christmas? Well, let me tell you. It has everything.

You see, Christmas jumpers are tasteless. And here's the thing. God is tasteless, too. That's actually the heart of the Good News. God is without a shred of cultural or aesthetic judgement. That must be so. It must be because God is a knitter too! The psalm presents God as carefully weaving us into being, knowing our every stitch and our every knot – knowing our depths and knowing our darkness and yet still being born among us in Jesus, still loving us. God has no taste. God does not discriminate. God does not exclude.

So wear that jumper with pride. You are fearfully and wonderfully made …

What do you find difficult to love about yourself? Ask God that you might see it through his eyes.

Holy God, in Mary's child you enter the world. You know us, yet you come to us – as one of us. You choose the least. You embrace the worst. And all for love of us. Amen.

30 DECEMBER
The Christmas Cake

God rained down upon them manna to eat ...
So mortals ate the bread of angels;
he sent them food in plenty.

Psalm 78.24, 25

We never know when to cut our Christmas cake. It would be unthinkable not to have one – its snow-white icing and glazed fruit glow so beautifully on the Christmas lunch table. But no one ever feels up to eating a slice! After turkey and pudding there is simply no room (just like that Bethlehem inn).

    I bake ours every year just before Advent. And then the fun begins – the weekly Sunday evening ritual of 'feeding' it. I unwrap it; I pierce it with tiny holes; I pour delicious Greek brandy over it; and I watch as it seeps into the cake. When we eventually get around to cutting it (rarely before 30 December) it tastes really amazing!

So, what's feeding you this Christmas week? Mince pies, naturally, but God offers God's people more than leftovers. In the wilderness God's people eat 'the bread of angels', the heavenly manna which sustains their bodies, but which is also a sign of God's unending faithfulness to them. God is faithful to us, too. God's faithfulness will endure when even the last crumb of cake has been eaten. It is a larder of love, a source of sustenance that will never fail us.

In the midst of the seasonal upheaval, what do you notice that is constant, enduring, and never-failing? How can it sustain you in the intense busy-ness of these days and the days ahead?

Holy God, in Mary's child you enter the world. You live among those whom you have always loved. You sustain them every moment with your enduring love. You can never let them go. In your faithfulness, we live. You are indeed our true feast. Amen.

NEW YEAR'S EVE
Falling Pine Needles

Every generous act of giving, with every perfect gift, is from above, coming down from the Father of lights, with whom there is no variation or shadow due to change.

James 1.17

I never enjoy New Year's Eve as much as I enjoy Christmas Eve. The prospect of the twelve days of Christmas is infinitely more joyful than the prospect of the twelve months of the New Year. Besides, much that has brought joy since Christmas Eve is looking jaded.

The floor is carpeted with fallen needles. The presents have been unwrapped. The fridge is nearly empty. I can't face another turkey sandwich. Honestly, a week on, it all feels a bit anticlimactic. So: where to find joy in the New Year that is almost here?

James reminds us that every generous act is a gift from God. Yes, the tree looks forlorn. No, there are no longer any presents underneath it. But stretching before us is a whole New Year. Dare we remember that in our God there is no shadow and no variation? Dare we remember that our God longs for one thing only – our flourishing? And dare we remember that God has gifted us 365 days, each of which offers us the opportunity of sharing God's gifts with others?

Because when we are generous to others, when we show love to others, when we seek the flourishing of others as God seeks our flourishing – then that's what we're doing. In our generosity, in our love, we are agents of the divine.

Write a list – a list of the people, the places, the moments in whom and in which the loving generosity of God becomes real for you. Treasure these.

Holy God, in Mary's child you enter the world. To the world we too are sent, to love as we are loved, to give as we have been given to, to reveal your longing for our flourishing. For this birth is good news for all people. Amen.

NEW YEAR'S DAY
Crackers (and Crowns)

From now on there is reserved for me the crown of righteousness, which the Lord ... will give to me.

2 Timothy 4.8

Christmas Day, or New Year's Day – what makes a good cracker? The gift, which must be useless enough to make you decide that crackers really are a waste of money. The snap, which must be loud enough to make you jump. The motto, which must be awful enough to make you groan. And the paper crown, which must be small enough (or big enough) to give you an excuse not to wear it.

The world receives a gift at Christmas, the gift of Mary's child. He arrives, not with a bang but with the new-born's shout of terror. The motto is sung by the herald angels, '*... on earth peace ...*' And the crown? Well, according to St Paul, that awaits those who long for Christ's appearing.

We may look for excuses not to wear this crown. Because we don't believe that it 'fits'. Because people might see it and judge us. Because we don't see the point of it.

But the child born in the dead of Christmas night embodies peace between humanity and divinity. He offers the crown of glory that never fades away to all who love him. That's the Christian faith. That's the Christian hope. It's a cracker! Happy New Year.

The angels sing ' *... on earth peace ...* '
What might be your motto for 2026
– for what do you long in this New Year?

Holy God, in Mary's child you enter the world. He is a gift beyond our imagining. Angels hymn the peace he brings, And, free from fear, we awaken to all he promises. Increase our longing for him; deepen our faith in him; build up our hope of him. Amen.

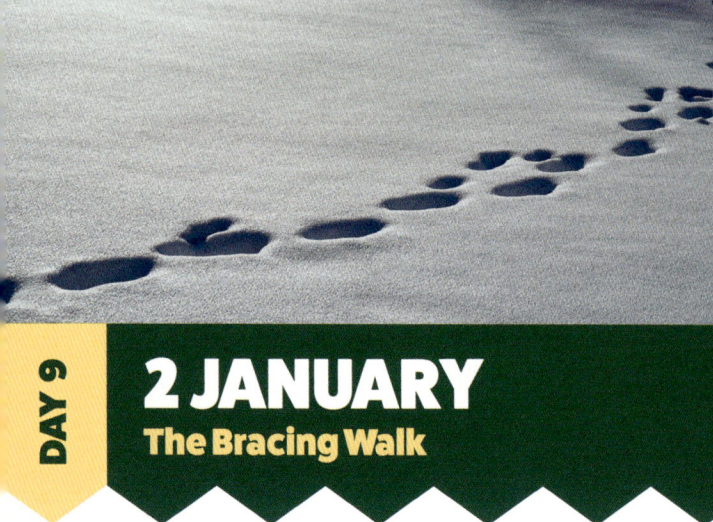

2 JANUARY
The Bracing Walk

Stand at the crossroads and look, and ask for the ancient paths, where the good way lies, and walk in it.

Jeremiah 6.16

I hope you've found time to stretch your legs and blow away the cobwebs? Gathering around the hearth to exchange gifts and good cheer is wonderful, but it can also be stifling (in every sense).

A walk means a change of scene, a breath of fresh air, a chance to work the muscles. But what route to take? Jeremiah's words resonate with anyone who has walked a historic woodland. At every crossroads there's a multiplicity of paths. The trampled bracken suggests that someone has blundered off to the left; a faint hint of marshy footprints, that someone has attempted to turn right; while ahead, a broad, well-trodden track beckons. 'Ask where the good way lies,' writes the prophet, 'and walk in it'.

One of the temptations of the New Year is that of self-reinvention. New hair, new job, new relationship: we blunder leftwards or attempt rightwards while all the time what we really need to do is rediscover the ancient path. The one mapped out for us at Christmas in the birth of Jesus – the path of self-giving, the path of self-forgetting, the path of faith and of love. Many have trodden it before us. All we have to do is follow.

In whose footsteps do you hope to walk this year? How will you remain faithful to the path?

Holy God, in Mary's child you enter the world. He shows us the way in which we must walk. We journey with him as our guide and companion. We journey with all who have journeyed before us. We discover that you are the journey's beginning and its end. Bless our journey, we pray. Amen.

3 JANUARY
A Season of Traditions

For now we see in a mirror, dimly, but then we will see face to face.

1 Corinthians 13.12

Christmas stockings may be opened before breakfast. Presents from under the tree may be opened only after the King's speech. That's correct, isn't it? Well, it is in our household.

It's the season of traditions, of well-worn rituals that are observed wordlessly every year. What games are played when. What films are watched when. We all have traditions: fine. Unless we fail to acknowledge that they are our traditions, and that others' may differ.

This is harder than it sounds. Each of us is shaped by a host of influences: when we were born, to whom we were born, what education we received. Our shaping is the only shaping we have experienced – it's not easy to remember that others (including those we love best) have had their own shaping. They will see differently and think differently. Not because they're being difficult. Because that's who they are.

It's a feature of Christmas life. It's a feature of Christian life. St Paul reminds us that humans '... see in a mirror, dimly'. We cannot hope to grasp the fullness of God – what we know will always be partial. Our neighbour will know God differently. That just might be an advantage – for us both.

How might our various traditions reveal God's love of difference?
What would be a practical way of showing love to (and learning from) those we don't agree with?

Holy God, in Mary's child you enter the world. Heaven stoops to Earth. Word is made flesh. We cannot understand this, but, through your grace, we will never stop learning. None of us. Keep us humbly mindful of that great truth. Amen.

4 JANUARY
Grandma's Greek Kitchen

May he come down like rain upon the mown grass,
like the showers that water the earth.

Psalm 72.6

On the Eleventh Day of Christmas I make *finikia* (if I haven't done so already). My father's family are from the Greek-speaking world, and, when we used to visit my grandparents in Cyprus, *finikia* were my favourite thing. Nowadays I make them at Christmas in my grandmother's honour – although mine will never be as good as hers.

    Finikia are soft-textured cakes flavoured with orange zest and spice and covered with chopped nuts. What makes them special is that when I take them out of the oven I drench them in a gorgeous syrup made with honey and freshly-squeezed lemon. *Oraia*, as the Greeks say.

Every day at the end of Advent we pray with today's verse from Psalm 72. It articulates the hope that God will be poured upon the earth as the rain is poured from the sky. What an amazing image! God's presence being tipped out upon us – not sparingly, in miserly quantities, but in glorious abundance, soaking us to our skin.

I repeat that verse as I pour hot syrup out upon my *finikia*. I watch it seeping into them and see them becoming suffused with it. I pray that as we celebrate his coming, we may be saturated with his gracious, loving presence.

What daily task might recall you to a Scriptural passage? Can you make of that task a prayer?

Holy God, in Mary's child you enter the world. Come to us this Christmas. Come like the rain. We seek no shelter from you. Fall upon us. Refresh us. Give us life. Amen.

5 JANUARY
The Unwanted Gift

Then, opening their treasure-chests, they offered him gifts of gold, frankincense, and myrrh.

Matthew 2.11

As I prepare to pack away the decorations for another year, I find a present that I haven't looked at since Christmas Day – because when I unwrapped it, I didn't like it, and I still don't. Why on earth did someone think I would want that?

History does not record what happened to the gifts brought by the Magi. On the face of it, gold, frankincense, and myrrh were not obvious presents for a baby born to a carpenter's family many miles from home. It seems unlikely that Jesus ever found a use for them. But we understand the gifts as prophetic symbols: they proclaim his identity as king, as priest, and as sacrificial offering. The Magi see something in the birth of Jesus that no one else sees.

As we collect together our unwanted gifts and end Christmas with a trip to the charity shop, perhaps it's worth looking through them and asking ourselves two questions. Does the giver of this gift not know me at all? Or do they know me better than I know myself?

The answer may be uncomfortable. But – once again – the birth of Mary's child will have brought us new knowledge of ourselves. Thanks be to God.

What has God given you in the course of these twelve days? Does it include anything unexpected – or unwelcome?
How might you make use of it in the New Year?

Holy God, in Mary's child you enter the world. We greet you as friend and brother. We hail you as Lord and Saviour. And we ask that as we grow in knowledge of you so may we grow in knowledge of ourselves as known, treasured, and beloved from eternity to eternity. Amen.

NEXT STEPS

We hope you have enjoyed these #TheJoyOfChristmas reflections

Here are some possible next steps on your journey:

Connect with God all year round with the Everyday Faith app. Journey daily with reflections like those in this booklet to inspire, equip and encourage you in your everyday faith. The app is free to download for iOS and Android via **cofe.io/EverydayFaithApp**

Find out more about the Christian faith and explore the key Christian texts – including The Lord's Prayer, the Commandments, and the Nicene Creed – via **cofe.io/WhatWeBelieve**

Join with others in worship and service at your local church. Find thousands of services and events, groups and activities taking place both on site and online all year round via **AChurchNearYou.com**

Build prayer into your day using the Daily Prayer app with audio. Visit **cofe.io/DailyPrayer** to join hundreds of thousands of people who have found daily calm and inspiration by making these services part of their rhythm of life.